ANTONIN DVOŘÁK

CELLO CONCERTO

B minor/h-Moll/Si mineur
Op. 104

Edited by/Herausgegeben von
Richard Clarke

Ernst Eulenburg Ltd

London · Mainz · Madrid · New York · Paris · Prague · Tokyo · Toronto · Zürich

CONTENTS

Ernst Eulenburg Ltd
48 Great Marlborough Street
London W1F 7BB

PREFACE

By the winter of 1891–2 Dvořák knew that he was soon to spend two years in America as Director of New York's National Conservatory of Music, and he made a farewell tour of Czechoslovakia performing his own music with a violinist and a cellist. For the occasion he wrote a rondo for cello and piano and arranged his piano duet, *Silent Woods* (Op. 68/5), for the same combination, and they were played by his friend Hanuš Wihan and himself. In New York in October 1893 he orchestrated the piano parts of both pieces. When he returned to his homeland the following summer for a few months he probably showed them to Wihan in their new form. He began work on a full-scale concerto for Wihan, an idea which already seems to have been developing in his mind, on 8 November 1894 in New York, during his last winter at the Conservatory; orchestration of the whole work was complete by 9 February 1895. Thoughts of home, however, can nevertheless be detected in this work and are particularly evident in the references to Czech folk music in the Finale.

The darkly modal gesture with which the clarinets announce the first movement, with its flattened leading-note, ushers in the first of the movement's two principal themes. This 'pure minor' mood suggestive of traditional idioms is common in Dvořák's music; though it appears prominently in his 'American' works (e.g. the 'New World' Symphony and the 'American' Quartet in F Op.96) through pentatonic scales and other folk-like melodic patterns, his style was characterized by similar inflections for many years before. There is a double exposition in this sonata-form movement – a classical convention of the concerto genre – in which the orchestra is first to present both main ideas. The second theme is a languorously beautiful melody for horn (bb57ff.), taken up by clarinet and rounded off with a rhythmic codetta hammered out in a punctuating tutti. The cello enters for a second exposition subtly brightening the disposition of the music with the D sharp of the tonic major. At the point where the recapitulation is expected, Dvořák reverses the order of his two themes following a brief central development. He brings in the horn's earlier melody, triumphantly usurping the place of the first subject, at which only hints are then made, rather than permitting again a complete revelation of its full identity.

While writing the slow movement, Dvořák heard with distress that his sister-in-law, Josefina Kaunitzová, was very ill, and this prompted him to quote from a song of his, *Leave me alone* (Op.82/1), of which Josefina had been especially fond. He changed the tune from 4/4 time to 3/4 (bb42ff.). By the end of April 1895 he was back in Prague, and a month later Josefina died. As some form of memorial to her, Dvořák revised the end of the Finale. He substituted 60 new bars (bb449ff.) in place of four bars in the original; they are among the loveliest he ever wrote. Thirty years earlier, in 1865, Dvořák had given her piano lessons and fallen in love with her; she refused him and he later married her younger sister. It may not be altogether a coincidence that in 1865 Dvořák was also writing a cello concerto; to some extent Josefina must have inspired both works. The earlier concerto, in A major, which he neither orchestrated nor tried to publish, was recovered from the estate of its dedicatee, the cellist Ludevit Peer, in 1925 and is now held at the British Library, London. Some attempt has been made to reconstruct a performing edition of this through-composed and somewhat diffuse 50-minute concerto.

In August 1895 Wihan played through the new B minor concerto with Dvořák at the piano and suggested a number of simplifications in the very difficult solo part. Not all of them appealed to the composer, who showed positive annoyance when Wihan tried to foist on him a cadenza he had written for insertion near the end of the Finale. Dvořák had clear reasons, it seems, for not wishing to disturb the flow of the closing moments of the third movement, since the final heroic gestures of its conclusion build up from veiled references to themes from the first two movements. He expressed his conception of the Finale in a letter to his publisher, Simrock, instructing them to publish the work as it had been originally conceived, largely without Wihan's emendations. However the simplifications shown in the first movement (bb261–5 and 327–40) and in the last (bb199–202) are presumably Wihan's.

The *Allegro moderato* Finale unfolds along an outwardly organic and oblique course, although this beguiling veneer conceals a subtly constructed rondo form. It broadly follows the pattern ABA'-CDC'-A"EA''', after the distant plod of marching horns in an introduction. Dvořák draws on Czech traditional idioms most obviously at first in the brief but sprightly B section (bb49–72) as well as in the more lyrically folk-like E section (bb281ff.). The two-bar motto that had opened the work, and which pervades the first movement (appearing even towards the end of the second movement at b124), is joined by a further suggestion of Josefina's song on a solo violin (bb468–473) before the concerto's confident dénouement. It is not, however, cyclic in the way that Elgar recalled the opening of his E minor Cello Concerto in its fourth movement, 20 or so years later; nevertheless, he and other composers of subsequent Cello Concertos have been indebted to the present work, including Shostakovich. Dvořák's Finale possesses a three-fold nostalgia: it recalls the work's opening, the composer's homeland through its music and, at a deeper level, the irretrievable loss of an early love.

By autumn 1895, Dvořák had been negotiating the first performance with the Philharmonic Society in London; when it proved difficult to find a date that suited Wihan he agreed after some resistance that the young cellist Leo Stern should be the soloist instead. He went through the solo part with Stern in Prague and conducted the first performance at the Queen's Hall in London on 19 March 1896. The cello used by Stern at the premiere, a 1684 Stradivarius named after General Kyd, who brought it to England in the 18th century, was famously stolen from a Los Angeles house in early 2004.

Notwithstanding a reservation expressed by the *Musical Times* immediately after the premiere ('We are by no means certain that this Violoncello Concerto will become a favourite. Dvořák has written soli that are covered up a good deal and eclipsed in interest by the orchestra'), the concerto has enjoyed unbroken favour with performers and audiences. Although for many years its difficulties seemed almost insurmountable, it is now in every cellist's repertoire. Wihan, to whom it is dedicated, did not play it until 1899, when Mengelberg conducted; he played it again in 1900 – in Budapest – this time, at long last, with Dvořák conducting. A notably poignant performance of the concerto took place in London at the BBC Proms on 21 August 1968, by Mstislav Rostropovich and the USSR Soviet Symphony Orchestra conducted by Yevgeny Vetlanov, the very same day that Soviet tanks rolled into Dvorak's homeland.

Roger Fiske (1975; updated 2011)

VORWORT

Im Winter des Jahres 1891–92 war es Dvořák schon bekannt, dass er in nächster Zukunft zwei Jahre als Direktor am New York National Conservatory of Music in Amerika verbringen würde, und so begab er sich, zusammen mit einem Geiger und einem Cellisten, die ihn beim Spielen seiner Musik unterstützen sollten, auf eine Abschiedstournee in der Tschechoslowakei. Zu diesem Anlass schrieb er ein Rondo für Violoncello und Klavier und arrangierte sein vierhändiges Stück *Waldesruhe* (Op. 68/5) für die gleichen Instrumente. Gespielt wurden diese Werke von seinem Freund Hanuš Wihan und ihm selbst. Im Oktober 1893 setzte er in New York die Klavierstimmen beider Stücke für Orchester. Als er im folgenden Sommer für einige Monate in sein Heimatland zurückkehrte, zeigte er sie vermutlich Wihan in ihrer neuen Fassung. Zu dieser Zeit trug er sich schon mit dem Gedanken, ein ganzes Konzert für Wihan zu schreiben. Wieder in New York, um dort seinen letzten Winter am Konservatorium zu verbringen, komponierte er das Konzert zwischen November 1894 und Februar 1895. Er sehnte sich damals danach, wieder zu Hause zu sein, und etwas von diesem Heimweh ist in der Musik zu spüren.

Der dunkle modale Gestus mit dem erniedrigten Leitton, mit dem die Klarinetten den ersten Satz eröffnen, leitet in das erste der beiden Hauptthemen ein. Diese „reine Moll-Stimmung", die an traditionelle Melodien erinnert, ist typisch für Dvořáks Musik. Obgleich sie hauptsächlich in seinen „amerikanischen" Werken (z. B. in der *Sinfonie Aus der Neuen Welt* und das *Amerikanische Quartett* in F, Op. 96) in Form von pentatonischen Skalen und anderen volkstümlichen Melodiemustern erscheint, war sein Stil seit vielen Jahren schon durch ähnliche Wendungen charakterisiert. In diesem Satz in Sonatenform gibt es eine doppelte Exposition – eine klassische Konvention in der Konzertliteratur – in der zuerst das Orchester beide Hauptthemen präsentiert. Das zweite Thema ist eine wunderschön sehnsuchtsvolle Melodie für Horn (Takt 57 ff.), die von der Klarinette übernommen und mit einer rhythmisch hämmernden Codetta im Tutti abgeschlossen wird. Das Cello tritt ein, führt eine zweite Exposition durch und hellt dabei die Stimmung durch ein „dis" der Dur-Tonika auf. An dem Punkt, an dem man die Reprise erwartet, stellt Dvořák die beiden Themen um und verbindet sie mit einer kurzen Durchführung. Er greift die frühere Horn-Melodie auf, die nun triumphierend den Platz des ersten Themas einnimmt. An das letztere erinnern nur noch Anklänge, anstatt dass Dvořák es ein weiteres Mal in aller Vollständigkeit präsentieren würde.

Während der Komposition des langsamen Satzes erfuhr Dvořák zu seinem Leidwesen, dass seine Schwägerin Josefina Kaunitzová schwer erkrankt sei, was ihn dazu veranlasste, aus dem von ihm komponierten Lied zu zitieren, das Josefina besonders gern hatte: *Lasst mich allein* (Op. 82/1). Doch machte er dabei aus dem Viertel- einen Dreivierteltakt (T. 42 ff.). Gegen Ende April 1895 war er wieder in Prag und Josefina starb einen Monat später. Dvořák änderte den Schluss des Finales in einer Art Gedenken an sie, indem er sechzig neue Takte anstelle der ursprünglichen vier setzte (T. 449 ff.). Sie gehören zu den schönsten, die er je geschrieben hat. 1865, also dreißig Jahre vorher, hatte Dvořák ihr Klavierunterricht gegeben und sich dabei in sie verliebt, doch hatte sie ihn zurückgewiesen. Später hatte er dann ihre jüngere Schwester geheiratet. Es mag nicht ganz zufällig gewesen sein, dass Dvořák auch im Jahre 1865 an einem Cellokonzert schrieb. Bis zu einem gewissen Grade muss Josefina beide Werke inspiriert haben. Das ältere Konzert in A-Dur, das er nie für Orchester gesetzt oder zu veröffentlichen versucht hat, wurde 1925 im Nachlass des Cellisten Ludevit Peer, dem es gewidmet war, wiederentdeckt. Heute wird es in der British Library aufbewahrt. Es hat einige Versuche gegeben, eine praktische Ausgabe dieses durchkomponierten und in gewisser Weise diffusen, 50 Minuten langen Konzerts herzustellen.

Im August 1895 spielte Wihan das Konzert in h-Moll mit Dvořák am Klavier durch und machte einige Vorschläge, welche die Vereinfachung gewisser Stellen in der sehr schwierigen Solostimme betrafen. Der Komponist fand nicht alle gut und ärgerte sich sogar recht über den Versuch Wihans, ihm eine selbstgeschriebene Kadenz zur Einfügung gegen Ende des Finales aufzudrängen. Es scheint, dass Dvořák klare Gründe dafür hatte, den musikalischen Fluss gegen Ende des dritten Satzes nicht unterbrechen zu wollen. Denn die den Satz beschließenden heroischen Wendungen basieren auf verschleierten Anklängen an Themen der ersten beiden Sätze. Er beschrieb seine Konzeption des Finales in einem Brief an seinen Verleger Simrock, den er anwies, das Werk so zu veröffentlichen, wie es ursprünglich konzipiert wurde, d. h. weitestgehend ohne Wihans Veränderungen. Die vereinfachten Fassungen im ersten (T. 261–65 und 327–41) und letzten Satz (T. 199–202) stammen indessen vermutlich von Wihan.

Das *Allegro moderato*-Finale entwickelt sich indirekt und nach außen organisch; allerdings verbirgt sich hinter dieser verführerischen Fassade eine fein konstruierte Rondo-Form. Sie folgt dabei, nach dem entfernten Stapfen marschierender Hörner in einer Einführung, weitgehend dem Schema ABA'-CDC'-A''EA'''. Dvořák greift im kurzen, aber lebhaften Abschnitt B (T. 49–72) sowie im lyrischeren, volkstümlichen Abschnitt E (T. 281ff.) zunächst ganz offenkundig auf traditionelle tschechische Ausdrucksformen zurück. Zu dem zweitaktigen Motto, mit dem das Werk eröffnet wurde und das den ersten Satz durchdringt (es erscheint sogar gegen Ende des zweiten Satzes in T. 124), gesellt sich vor dem souveränen Ausgang des Konzerts eine weitere Anspielung auf Josefinas Lied auf einer Solovioline (T. 468–473). Es ist jedoch nicht auf dieselbe Art und Weise zyklisch, auf die Elgar ungefähr zwanzig Jahre später den Beginn seines Cellokonzerts in e-Moll in dessen viertem Satz ins Gedächtnis ruft; trotzdem waren er und andere

Komponisten nachfolgender Cellokonzerte, einschließlich Schostakowitsch, dem vorliegenden Werk verpflichtet. Dvořáks Finale ist dreifach nostalgisch: Es erinnert an den Beginn des Werks, an die Heimat des Komponisten und auf einer tieferen Ebene an den Verlust einer frühen Liebe.

Im Herbst 1895 verhandelte Dvořák mit der Philharmonic Society in London über die Erstaufführung und als sich herausstellte, dass ein passendes Datum für Wihan schwer zu finden war, erklärte sich Dvořák nach einigem Widerstand damit einverstanden, den jungen Cellisten Leo Stern an seiner Stelle als Solisten anzunehmen. In Prag ging er die Solostimme mit Stern durch und in der Londoner Queen's Hall dirigierte er dann die Erstaufführung am 19. März 1896. Das Violoncello, das Stern bei der Erstaufführung spielte, ein Stradivari, das nach dem General Kyd benannt ist, der es im 18. Jahrhundert nach England gebracht hatte, wurde Anfang 2004 Opfer eines spektakulären Raubs in einem Haus in Los Angeles.

Ungeachtet der Vorbehalte, die kurz nach der Uraufführung in der *Musical Times* zum Ausdruck gebracht wurden („Wir sind uns keinesfalls sicher, dass dieses Violoncello-Konzert Beliebtheit erlangen wird. Dvořák schrieb Soli, die zu einem großen Teil überdeckt und durch ein zu großes Interesse am Orchester in den Hintergrund gedrängt werden"), erfreut sich das Konzert ungebrochener Beliebtheit bei Ausführenden und Hörern. Obgleich die technischen Schwierigkeiten für Jahre als unüberwindbar angesehen wurden, gehört das Werk heute zum Repertoire eines jeden Cellisten. Wihan, dem es gewidmet ist, hat es selbst erst 1899 unter Mengelberg gespielt. 1900 spielte er es wieder in Budapest, diesmal endlich unter Dvořáks Leitung. Eine besonders ergreifende Aufführung des Konzerts fand am 21. August 1968 in London bei den BBC Proms mit Mstislav Rostropowitsch und dem Sowjetischen Sinfonieorchester der UdSSR unter der Leitung von Jewgeny Wetlanow statt, genau an dem Tag, als sowjetische Panzer in Dvořáks Heimatland einrückten.

Roger Fiske (1975, aktualisiert 2011)

PRÉFACE

Au cours de l'hiver 1891/92, Dvořák, informé de son départ imminent vers l'Amérique où il occupera les fonctions de directeur du Conservatoire national de musique de New York pendant deux ans, fit une tournée d'adieu en Tchécoslovaquie au cours de laquelle il donna certaines de ses œuvres en compagnie d'un violoniste et d'un violoncelliste. Il écrivit pour l'occasion un *rondo* pour violoncelle et piano, arrangea *Bois silencieux* (Op.68/5), à l'origine pour piano à quatre mains, pour la même formation et interpréta ces pièces avec son ami, le violoncelliste Hanuš Wihan. Il orchestra les parties de piano de ces deux œuvres à New York en 1893 et en soumit probablement cette nouvelle version à Wihan l'été suivant, alors qu'il séjournait quelques mois dans son pays. De retour à New York pour son dernier hiver à la tête du Conservatoire, il commença, dès le 8 novembre 1894, le concerto entier pour violoncelle dont l'idée avait, semble-t-il, déjà cheminé dans son esprit et qu'il destina à Wihan. L'orchestration complète en fut achevée le 9 février 1895. On y relève plusieurs évocations de son pays natal, particulièrement évidentes dans les références à la musique traditionnelle tchèque du *Finale*.

L'inflexion modale sombre, à la note sensible bémolisée, par laquelle les clarinettes annoncent le premier mouvement introduit les deux thèmes principaux. Cette ambiance de « mineur pur » rappelant les modes ancestraux, qui imprégnait le style de Dvořák depuis de nombreuses années, colora de manière marquée ses œuvres « américaines » (Symphonie *Nouveau monde* et Quatuor en *fa* « *Américain* », Op.96, entre autres) par le truchement de gammes pentatoniques et d'autres motifs mélodiques traditionnels. Ce mouvement en forme sonate – convention classique du genre du concerto – comporte une double exposition dans laquelle l'orchestre énonce le premier les deux idées principales. Le deuxième thème consiste en une belle mélodie langoureuse jouée par le cor (mes. 57 et suiv.), reprise par la clarinette et terminée par une *codetta* rythmée ponctuée d'un *tutti* martelé. L'entrée du violoncelle pour la deuxième exposition éclaircit subtilement le tissu musical par l'apparition du *ré* dièse de la tonalité majeure de tonique. Au moment de la réexposition, Dvořák inverse l'ordre de ses deux thèmes après un bref développement central et réintroduit la mélodie de cor précédemment entendue qui prend triomphalement la place du premier thème, celui-ci étant simplement évoqué plus que totalement réinstallé dans son identité propre.

Très peiné à l'annonce de la grave maladie dont était atteinte sa belle-sœur, Josefina Kaunitzová, tandis qu'il travaillait à la composition du mouvement lent, Dvořák y cita une de ses mélodies, *Laisse-moi seul* (Op. 82/1), que Josefina affectionnait particulièrement, transformant la mesure à 4/4 en mesure à 3/4 (mes. 42 et suiv.). Rentré à Prague fin avril 1895, un mois avant la mort de Josefina, Dvořák retravailla la conclusion du *Finale* en hommage à celle-ci. Il substitua, aux quatre mesures de la première version, soixante nouvelles mesures (mes. 449 et suiv.) qui se placent parmi les plus belles qu'il ait jamais écrites. Quelques trente années auparavant, en 1865, Dvořák s'était épris de Josefina, à laquelle il donnait des leçons de piano, mais celle-ci le repoussa et il épousa plus tard sa jeune sœur. Le fait que Dvořák travaillait déjà à un concerto pour violoncelle en 1865 n'est peut-être pas une simple coïncidence. Il se peut que Josefina ait, d'une certaine façon, inspiré les deux œuvres. La partition de ce premier concerto en *la* majeur, qu'il n'orchestra jamais, ni n'essaya de publier et qui fut retrouvée en 1925 parmi les biens de son dédicataire, le violoncelliste Ludevit Peer, est actuellement conservée à la British Library et a fait l'objet d'une tentative de reconstitution de ce concerto de cinquante minutes, entièrement composé et quelque peu diffus, dont une édition d'exécution a été établie.

En août 1895, Wihan déchiffra la partition du nouveau concerto en *si* mineur, accompagné par Dvořák au piano, et suggéra un certain nombre de simplifications dans la partie très complexe du soliste. Toutes ne furent pas du goût du compositeur, qui exprima son franc désaccord lorsque Wihan tenta de lui imposer une cadence qu'il avait écrite en vue de l'insérer au terme du *Finale*. Dvořák avait, semble-t-il, de bonnes raisons de ne pas vouloir interrompre le flux des dernières mesures du troisième mouvement dont la bravoure conclusive s'appuie sur des allusions voilées à des thèmes issus des deux premiers mouvements. Il expliqua sa conception du *Finale* dans une lettre adressée à son éditeur Simrock, lui recommandant de publier l'œuvre telle qu'elle avait été conçue à l'origine et d'ignorer certaines des variantes de Wihan. Toutefois, les modifications rencontrées dans le premier mouvement (mes. 261–265 et 327–340) et dans le troisième mouvement (mes. 199–202) sont vraisemblablement dues à Wihan.

L'*Allegro moderato* final se déroule selon un parcours apparemment spontané et dénué de direction visible, or ce vernis trompeur dissimule une forme *rondo* dont la structure est élaborée sur le schéma ABA -CDC -A EA , après une introduction constituée par la marche distante et pesante des cors. Dvořák y reprend des tournures traditionnelles tchèques, surtout dans la section B, brève et enjouée (mes. 49–72), ainsi que dans la section E, plus lyrique et folklorique (mes. 281 et suiv.). Le motif initial de deux notes qui se dissémine dans tout le premier mouvement (il apparaît même vers la fin du deuxième mouvement à la mesure 124) rejoint une nouvelle évocation de la mélodie de Josefina par un solo de violon (mesures 468– 473) avant le dénouement confiant du concerto. Cette œuvre n'est pas cyclique au sens où, vingt ans plus tard, Elgar rappela le début de son concerto pour violoncelle en *mi* mineur dans son quatrième mouvement. Ce dernier et d'autres compositeurs de concertos pour violoncelle ensuite, y compris Chostakovitch, furent toutefois redevables de l'influence de l'œuvre de Dvořák dont le *Finale* déploie une triple nostalgie par le rappel du début de l'œuvre, par l'évocation de son pays natal et, à un niveau plus enfoui, par le souvenir de la perte irréversible d'un amour ancien.

A l'automne 1895, Dvořák discuta de la création de l'œuvre à Londres avec la Philharmonic Society. Devant la difficulté de trouver une date qui convienne à Wihan, Dvořák accepta, après quelques réticences, que la partie de soliste fût confiée au jeune violoncelliste Leo Stern. Il travailla la partition avec Stern à Prague et dirigea la première exécution du concerto à Londres, au Queen's Hall, le 19 mars 1896. Le violoncelle que joua Stern à cette occasion, un Stradivarius de 1684, nommé d'après le Général Kyd qui l'avait apporté en Angleterre au XVIIIème siècle, fit l'objet d'un vol célèbre à Los Angeles en 2004.

En dépit de la réserve exprimée par le *Musical Times* dès sa création (« Nous ne sommes en aucun cas certains de la postérité de ce Concerto pour violoncelle. Les *soli* écrits par Dvořák sont souvent recouverts par l'orchestre qui les éclipse »), ce concerto a connu un succès ininterrompu auprès des interprètes et des publics. Pendant de longues années, les difficultés qu'il présente parurent insurmontables, mais il fait maintenant partie du répertoire de tout violoncelliste. Wihan, à qui il est dédié, ne le joua pour la première fois qu'en 1899, sous la direction de Mengelberg, puis – enfin sous la direction de Dvořák – en 1900 à Budapest. Mstislav Rostropovitch, avec l'Orchestre symphonique soviétique de l'URSS sous la direction de Yevgény Vetlanov, en donna une exécution notoirement poignante aux BBC Proms de Londres le 21 août 1968, le jour de l'invasion par les chars soviétiques de la patrie de Dvořák.

Roger Fiske (1975; actualisé en 2011)

CELLO CONCERTO

Hanusi Wihanovi

Antonín Dvořák
(1841–1904)
Op. 104

I. Allegro ♩ = 116

Edited by Richard Clarke
© 2011 Ernst Eulenburg Ltd, London
and Ernst Eulenburg & Co GmbH, Mainz

4

Quasi improvisando

14

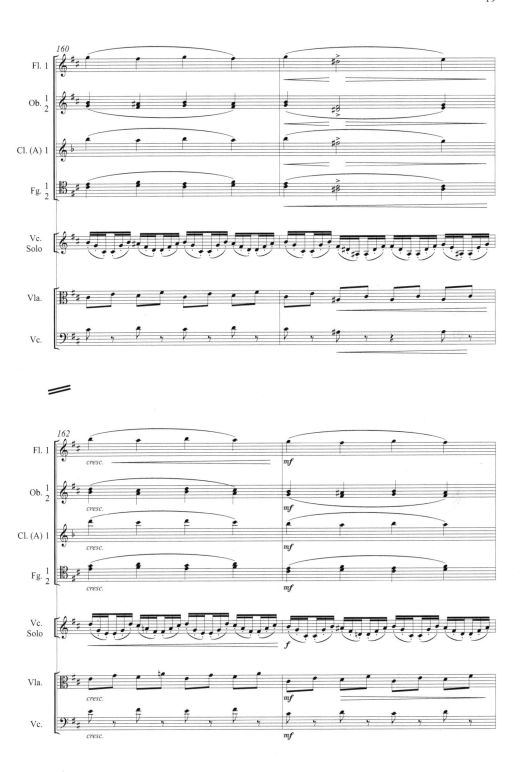

molto ritard. 8 **Grandioso**

poco ritard.

10 **Molto sostenuto** ($\quarternote = 100$)
in tempo

Animato

14

46

II. Adagio ma non troppo ♪ = 108

55

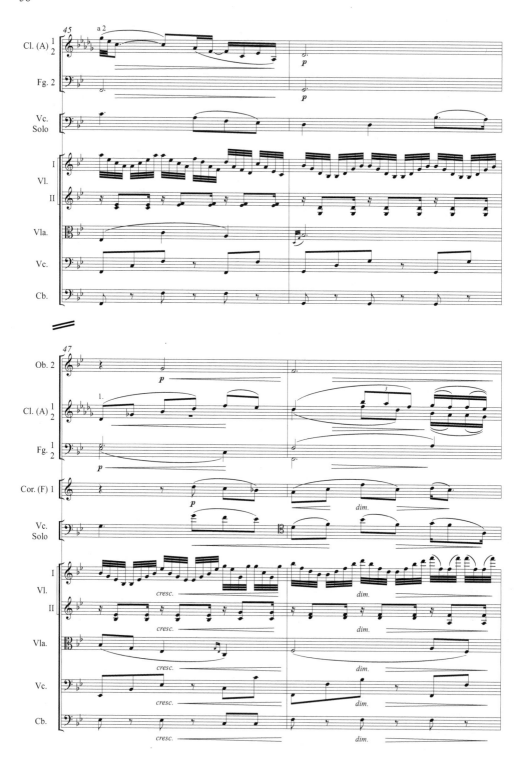

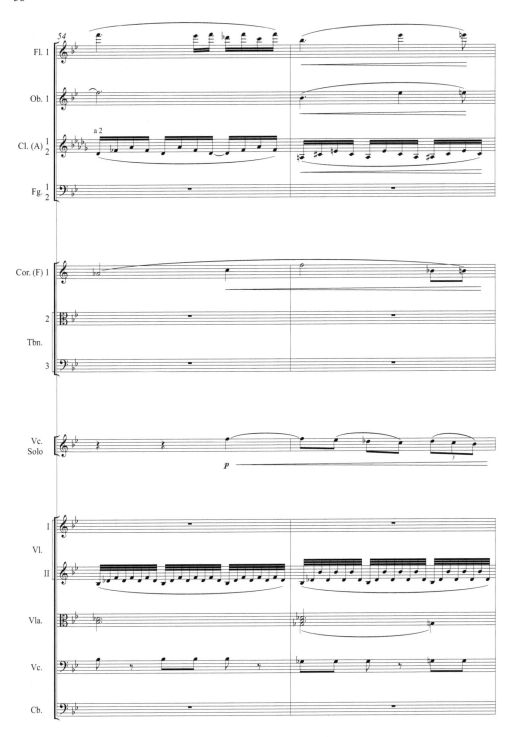

Un poco più animato

poco a poco ritard.

4 **Meno. Tempo I**

Un poco più animato

poco a poco string.

poco a poco rit.

74

poco a poco accel.

Tempo I ♩ = 104

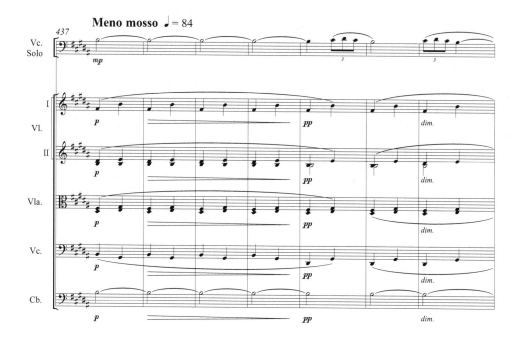